DOUBLE MINDEDNESS

CHERYL T. LONG

Dedication

This book is dedicated to "Self-Love" because "Self-Love" is the greatest love of all!!!

Acknowledgments

First and foremost I would like to thank God. In the course of putting this book together, I appreciated how true this gift of writing is for me. You've given me the power to believe in my passion and follow my dreams. I could never have done this without the faith I have in you, the Almighty.

To my Mom and Dad Elizabeth and Kenneth: "For the first time in 40 years, I am speechless! I can barely find the words to express all the wisdom, love and support you've given me. You are my #1fans, and for that, I am eternally grateful."

To my children, Devon, Anjanae, Shinera and Robyn: "You are the best thing that I have ever done in my life! You welcomed me into motherhood, and I am so grateful for all of you. Mommy loves you more than you will ever know and my writing is proof of the beauty I see whenever I look into your eyes, know this!"

TABLE OF CONTENTS

INTRODUCTION.. 1

CHAPTER ONE 4

Get Real! Don't Be Double 4

CHAPTER TWO 9

Characteristics of a Double-Minded Believer..................... 9

CHAPTER THREE 13

Renewing Your Mind 13

CHAPTER FOUR... 21

The Danger of Double-mindedness 21

CHAPTER FIVE 27

Single-Mindedness Vs. Double-Mindedness..................... 27

CONCLUSION 34

About Author 35

More Books by the Author... 36

INTRODUCTION

E ver had double vision when your brain sees one picture twice, overlapping and leaving you disoriented? James said that we can be double-visioned or double-minded (literally, "double-souled") in our relationship with God. When we pray or think about the Lord, a conflicting thought or picture such as lust for money or distaste for God's providence may enter into our minds. Suddenly, a real contest arises over which vision we prefer. Doubts, which possess the multiplier effect, produce a double-minded soul that poses a serious challenge to our faith. Double-mindedness blows cold air on a flaming heart. Jesus spoke of this danger in (Matthew 6:24); He likened it to the possibility of serving two masters, which he termed — impossible. James further expanded Jesus' warning that doubt and double-mindedness make us "unstable in all of our ways" (James 1:8). You can study James 1 for better understanding.

CAUSES OF DOUBLE-MINDEDNESS

According to commentator Douglas J. Moo, James was probably addressing previous members of his congregation in Jerusalem, who had fled from Israel due to religious persecutions (Acts 11:19). James called these souls the "dispersed" (James 1:1) — those separated from the mother church in Jerusalem due to persecutions (Isaiah 49:6; 1 Peter 1:1). "Dispersed" is a crucial term used to grasp the most out of James' exhortation. These believers had become strangers in a foreign land, a situation similar to their ancestors' exile in Assyria or Babylonia. Being dispersed in a spiritually hostile territory opens the door to bewilderment, doubt over God's providence, and temptations to adopt habits of the new neighbors. It can provide an alternative picture that divides the mind over religion. Today, many Christians voluntarily disperse or separate themselves from the visible church. As they lack the grace of reading and preaching the Word, the sacraments and prayer; they begin to think of alternative definitions of the church or extra biblical ways to be the church. They become double-minded about the church.

James 1:2 tells us to be joyful when we fall into various trials. When saints undergo tests, there is a picture that God wants to be formed in their minds so that they may be steadfast (v. 3–4). Without this picture as they go through trials, their prayers are coupled with lack of wisdom, and doubts cloud their thinking, and competes with a correct view of God (v. 5–6). They lose assurance that God would hear their prayers (v. 7). They become double-minded (v. 8) and unstable spiritually.

Verse 14 explains that all believers on earth live in yet-unredeemed bodies that are capable of being deceived about God (see v. 16), and we have professing Christians who are double-minded persons and experience the battle of allegiances.

CHAPTER ONE

Get Real! Don't Be Double

The reality is that many of us lead double lives most of the time. I'm not talking about the obvious things like being civil to someone you don't like or professing enjoyment when you're bored to tears. No, our double lives go deeper. We need to recognize it and need to get real. Let me explain.

On most Sunday mornings, we head to the church (whether it's a building, a TV station or online) to hear the Truth of God's Word. For about an hour or two, we sing praise songs, profess our love to God, listen to Biblical teaching and we are reminded that He is all-powerful, ever-present and in control. Our Sunday worship time is when we get really immersed in the presence of God.

Then we hit the rest of the week, forgetting that God's Word is just as true on Tuesday or Friday as it was on Sunday morning. On such days that challenges our faith, we forget His Lordship and allow the world to dictate the so-called "reality" of our circumstances. God calls this lifestyle double-mindedness. Furthermore, He says that a double-minded man is unstable (James 1:8) and should not expect to receive anything of the Lord (v. 7). Why? Because it is faith that connects us to His Blessing and grace, therefore, to receive from the Lord, a life of faith is essential.

For instance, we hear "I am the Lord that healeth thee," then we go to the doctor in faith, expecting the good news of healing that God has already promised. If the report is bad, we let fear and anger terrorize us instead of casting down imaginations and every high thing that exalts itself against the knowledge of God and taking every thought captive to the obedience of Christ (2 Cor. 10:5). Standing in faith is the critical difference between victory and defeat. Note that taking our thoughts captive is considered as obedience to the Lord, Jesus Christ. As our Lord, we owe Him allegiance, trusting His word as the law of our lives.

Now, I'm not saying we should ignore the medical profession. Those dedicated individuals are one of the blessings that God provides to keep His people well. After all, Apostle Luke was a physician. Instead, we should stand in faith, praying that they will be led by the wisdom and inspiration of Christ; "*praying always with all prayer and supplication in the Spirit, being watchful to this end with all perseverance and supplication for all the saints*" (Eph.

6:18). This is when we need to take hold of God's promises as the final authority in our lives and not let it go!

I'll admit: it is very easy to let the world and its constant barrage of bad news dictate our thoughts, words and feelings, but that is not how God want us to live. He declared several times in His Word, "*the just shall live by faith.*" Even stronger, Paul taught that without faith it is impossible to please Him! (Heb.11:6). Many people think it's impossible to please God. They think He is just watching and waiting for us to do something wrong or screw up in some way. But that's not true neither is it the case. The second half of that verse in Hebrews says, *"For he that cometh to God must believe that He is, and that He is a rewarder of those who diligently seek Him."* God always rewards faith.

The latter part of Psalm 35:27 says, *"God has pleasure in the prosperity of His servant."* In church, we hear that verse and think, "Yeah! God wants to bless me!" But by Tuesday, the bills pile up and we wonder, "Does God really care? Will He really do anything for me?" Our double-mindedness caused us to forget the promise of 1 Peter 5:7 that says, *"cast all your cares on Him for what He cares for you."*

The next verse advises: *"Be sober, be vigilant, because your adversary, the devil, walks about as a roaring lion, seeking whom he may devour."* How does he try to devour you? He does this by putting doubts in your mind; therefore, you begin to question the promises of God. Satan wants you to be double-minded because it sabotages your faith and weakens your effectiveness against his ploys.

Listen to the Great Physician's words as He appeared to His followers after His resurrection: *"Why are ye troubled, and why do thoughts arise in your hearts?"* (Luke. 24:38) Even though they had travelled with Him for three years, they let their faith slide away because of the present circumstances (crucifixion and burial of Jesus). They became double-minded — recalling Jesus' teachings but doubting their truth.

It is essential for us to get really determined to trust and obey God's Word regardless of what may be happening in the world. 1 Chronicles 28:9b says, *"...for the Lord searcheth all hearts and understandeth all the imaginations of thy thoughts. If thou seek Him, He will be found by thee; but if thou forsake Him, He will cast thee off forever."* The end of that verse sounds cruel, but it's not His choice; it is our choice to choose whether to be faithful or fearful. We can either choose to be consistent in our faith or allow our thoughts to become double-minded.

Let's get really devoted to building our faith by committing to walk by the Word, and preventing satan from controling our lives. After all, we are citizens of the Kingdom and members of the household of God (Eph. 2:19), seated in heavenly places in Christ Jesus (Eph. 2:6) and joint heirs with Him (Rom. 8:17). We have been given the Word (John 17:14), the measure of faith (Rom. 12:3) and His divine power that gives us all things that pertain unto life and godliness, through the knowledge of Him that has called us to glory and virtue (2 Peter 1:3). This is what the "real" you can get!

CHAPTER TWO

Characteristics of a Double-Minded Believer

1) There are two major influences that fuel your thought life.

A double-minded Christian is always being torn into two directions; he has a relationship with Jesus Christ as his Lord and Savior, and also has a relationship with a particular sinful obsession. It is a mental obsession and distraction, and it may even have a physical effect. This is a miserable way to attempt to live the Christian life; you will not enjoy the fullness that comes with it.

2) You have a history with both of your major influences.

No Christian becomes double-minded overnight; it takes some time to develop an unrelenting desire to pursue a particular course. But make no mistake about it, history has a way of repeating itself. Until we part ways with that thing that "stabs Jesus" all the time, we will continually find ourselves in a state of inner turmoil. Even if you have walked with the Lord for years, a double-minded life will circumvent much of the good the Holy Spirit wants to work in you and through you. What every believer desperately needs is to fully surrender their heart and mind to their Lord.

3) You find yourself compromising your thought life in one primary area.

Satan has been at his craft for many centuries, and just as he knew what "triggers" to employ with Adam and Eve, he has discovered a variety of enticements that are intended to lead believers to become double-minded. Satan hates to see believers fully surrendered to the Lord. The devil knows from the past experience that when a Christian is fully surrendered, God works more miracles through him in the lives of His people. Jesus has never compromised but can the same be said about us? Our challenge as sinful human beings is saying "no" to sin and "yes" to righteous living. This challenge not only confronts us once or twice a week; the temptations for compromise goes on around us all the time.

4) You are led by the Holy Spirit, except when that other issue is driving your thinking.

A Christian led by the Spirit cannot be compromise, instead, he or she is focused, filled, and flowing in the living water of the Holy Spirit. It is a wonderful way to go through life. It provides peace, power and purpose. Sin, on the other hand, fuels the desire to give into temptation again, and again — you never get enough. Therefore, you end up being double-minded, at least until you repent and come "clean" before the Lord and His cross.

5) You only experience real peace in your heart when your mind is under God's control.

There is no peace for the believer who is going against his conscience and against the word of God; he feels out of control. He feels pulled in the direction of obsession, rather than being led gently down the flowing river of God's grace and peace. Most of us who have known the Lord for a while have come to experience the vast difference between the peace of God and the turmoil of our sinful desires. They truly are in conflict with each other (see Gal. 5:16,17), and it's a battle that doesn't stop until the soul leaves the body at the point of physical death. At that moment, we will be immediately ushered into heaven.

6) You find yourself giving into old habits very easily.

A double-minded believer finds it next to impossible to stay away from the danger zone; he or she moves quickly in that direction at the slightest impulse. The longer a person refrains from that bad habit, the easier it gets to stay away from it; but the more you "cut corners," the more you find yourself locked into a double-minded quagmire of your own making. God's Word says that a double-minded man is "unstable in all he does" (James 1:8); this is why old habits seem to hang on indefinitely in the life of a double-minded believer. Those old habits are simply the fruit of an unstable heart and mind.

7) You would love to be drawn only to the things of God.

Deep within the soul of every believer is the desire to live fully for God. That desire was planted inside us when we were converted through faith in Christ. At that moment, the Holy Spirit took up residence within our body, and we immediately began to experience this righteous desire to do things in God's way. That desire will always be there within the soul of a Christian, even if you are double-minded. But the only way to experience the joy and peace that God intends for us is to get back to a single-minded approach of a Christian life (just like when you first came to know Christ). By His grace, you can get back there. After all, it was only His grace that brought you into this relationship in the first place.

CHAPTER THREE

Renewing Your Mind

As a child I loved Jesus very much, but other things became more important as I became older. There were many influences from friends, which in turn helped me to be defiant.

I grew up in a house where God was not only alive, but also revered. I was taught things like "Don't cheat, don't lie, don't steal, show respect to others, respect your elders." We went to church every Sunday. The name of God was always spoken. However, no one taught us about the challenges of double-mindedness.

The subconscious mind controls how you respond to everything in your life; it has a significant impact not only on your happiness but also on your ability to manifest the life God wishes for you.

I was torn between wanting to be a Christian and wanting

to go against God's word.

It was as if I had two minds; all of my attention was channeled into internal battles, challenges, and defeats, followed by attempts to repent and behave differently. As Christians, we do this sometimes.

No man can serve two masters, but I secretly preferred to remain the way I had been for years because it was comfortable. It's almost a part of who I am.

I was deceiving myself; I didn't see anything wrong with skipping church on the flimsiest of justifications. When I was in trouble, I would read my bible. I used to treat God like a pastime. I was so sick and tired of being mentally sick.

That's when I made up my mind on who I'd like to serve. I was tired of being insecure, because a person with two minds is insecure in every way.

My flesh initially refused to yield to Jesus, and it rebelled and went on a rampage for months. I litterally had temper tantrums from time to time.

I went through a variety of withdrawal symptoms.

We can learn by reading and putting God's laws into practice. We should work hard to see our minds as future partners rather than adversaries. The mind serves an important function and can provide you with unique knowledge that should be cherished rather than dismissed.

As a result, instead of hammering my subconscious into submission, I'm gentle with myself as I apply the strategies I've learned from God's word and God's way.

See below:

2 Corinthians 10:4-6 says, "For the weapons of our warfare are not carnal but mighty in God for pulling down strongholds, casting down arguments and every high thing that exalts itself against the knowledge of God, bringing every thought into captivity to the obedience of Christ, and being ready to punish all disobedience when your obedience is fulfilled."

Satan's strongholds are thoughts. If the devil can get you to entertain his thoughts, fear, anxiety, doubt, apprehension, and so on, he can have a doorway into controlling your mind. He will put a ring in your nose and lead you around if you entertain those thoughts, but we don't have to let him to this. The Word of God tells us how to be victorious; it shows us how to be more than conquerors in Him who loved us and gave Himself for us.

James 4:6-8 says, *"But He gives more grace. Therefore He says: "God resists the proud, but gives grace to the humble." Therefore submit to God. Resist the devil and he will flee from you. Draw near to God and He will draw near to you. Cleanse your hands, you sinners; and purify your hearts, you double-minded."* Trying to resist the devil without doing the rest of what this Word says is to be taking it out of context. Verse. 8 says "Draw near to God and He will draw near to you. Cleanse your hands, you sinners; and purify your hearts, you double-minded." Double-mindedness is another way of saying you are wishy-washy when it comes to what you believe, or that you are not settled in your spirit that the Word of God is true. There is a cure for that; find out what God's Word has to say, hear it, meditate on it, and let it take root in your spirit. Only then will faith arise in your heart.

Romans 10:17 says, *"So then faith comes by hearing, and hearing by the word of God."* Double-mindedness is quoting the Word of God with your mouth and not really expecting it to come to pass; you are allowing doubt and unbelief to be your ruler. Romans 10: 9-10 says, *"if you confess with your mouth the Lord Jesus and believe in your heart that God has raised Him from the dead, you will be saved. For with the heart one believes to righteousness, and with the mouth confession is made to salvation."* If you really don't believe God's Word, but you think that having a good confession concerning whatever you desire will make it come to pass — you're amiss.

Fear, doubt, anxiety, and other tools of the devil come to us through our mind. To try to stand against such things without mind renewal with the Word of God will cause us to fail and have a defeated attitude. In order to appropriate the victory given to us by the Lord Jesus Christ, we must first renew our minds with the Word of God, and begin to look at ourselves as God looks at us.

Psalms 1:2-3 says *"But his delight is in the law of the Lord, And in His law he meditates day and night. He shall be like a tree planted by the rivers of water, That brings forth its fruit in its season, Whose leaf also shall not wither; And whatever he does shall prosper."* If we confess the Word of God and be steadfast in it and not double-minded, we will see the end result of it.

Many times we know what the Word of God says about different areas of life and may see some corresponding victories in those areas, but when the outward circumstances do not agree with the Word of God; we tend to think that our faith failed, and we get discouraged therefore allowing condemnation to come in from the enemy. This is truly the trial of our faith, we must make a choice to stand up for what we believe, either the circumstances of our life or the Word of God. I know that it is not always easy to bring your thought life into captivity to the obedience of Christ, but God's Word tells us to do it, therefore we can. We cannot do it by our own power or by the strength of our own intellect. A Christian cannot lead a victorious life except by the anointing of God's Word and the power of the Holy Spirit, therefore, we have to study the Word of God first, and then lean on the Spirit of God for our strength.

John 6:63 says, *"It is the Spirit who gives life; the flesh profits nothing. The words that I speak to you are spirit, and they are life."* We must allow God's Word by the power of the Holy Spirit to charge our spirits until our spirit dominates our mind and flesh, else, the world and the devil will join forces to defeat us. By allowing our born again spirits to be empowered by the Word of God to dominate our mind, we can bring it into subjection to God's Word and stand victorious when all hell is coming against us. Then, the devil cannot toss us around with doubtful thoughts, nor discouragements, nor gain supremacy over us. When a Christian learns that the circumstances of life does not in any way show where he or she is spiritually, he or she will rejoice. Also, when we learn that our recreated human spirit can be masters of our intellect and senses, we can have a strong and constant faith.

Romans 8:6 *"For to be carnally minded is death, but to be spiritually minded is life and peace."* Spiritual mindedness is much more than just thinking about Heaven: it is preventing your mind from being swayed by circumstances or doubtful thoughts; it is by putting your mind under submission to the Word of God. By constantly dwelling on God's Word and meditating on His precepts, we bring our mind into submission to God's will. God's Word is God's will. When we renew our mind to the level where doubts has no room, the power of faith can be released and Godly results will be obtained.

Satan loves to attack the thought and lives of Christians. He batters Christians with thoughts of fear, anxiety, worry, sickness, defeat, and death. But we can be victorious in Jesus

Christ; for He has shown us how to be.

We opened up with 2 Corinthians 10:4-5 which says, *"For the weapons of our warfare are not carnal (or mental) but mighty in God for pulling down strongholds, casting down arguments and every high thing that exalts itself against the knowledge of God, bringing every thought into captivity to the obedience of Christ."* We have a part to play in our victory; we must make use of our weapons of warfare. God will not use them for us. Renewing our mind is a continuous process, we must die to "self" daily and continually keep our mind under subjection to what God's Word is saying. This means we have to feed on God's Word continually to become strong. When negative thoughts come, and they will, we have been given the tools to deal with them. Philippians 4:8 says, *"Finally, brethren, whatever things are true, whatever things are noble, whatever things are just, whatever things are pure, whatever things are lovely, whatever things are of good report, if there is any virtue and if there is anything praiseworthy meditate on these things."*

The first step is knowing for sure that you have eternal life. If you want to know for sure that you are a child of God, then earnestly pray this prayer.

Dear Heavenly Father, I come to you in the name of Jesus. Your word says, "*...and the one who comes to Me I will by no means cast out.*" (John 6:37), so I know You won't cast me out but take me in, and I thank you for it. You said in your Word, "*whoever calls upon the name of the Lord shall be saved.*" (Romans 10:13). I am calling on Your name, so I know You have saved me now, You also said, "*...that if you confess with your mouth the Lord Jesus and believe in your heart that God has raised Him from the dead, you will be saved. For with the heart one believes to righteousness, and with the mouth confession is made to salvation.*" (Romans 10:9–10).

I believe in my heart that Jesus Christ is the Son of God; I believe He was raised from the dead for my justification. And I confess Him now as my Lord, because Your Word says, "*...with the heart one believes to righteousness...*" and I do believe with my heart, I have now become the righteousness of God in Christ. (2 Corinthians 5:21).

And I am saved! Thank You, Lord! I can now truthfully say that, I see myself as a born again child of God! Glory be to God! Amen.

CHAPTER FOUR

The Danger of Double-mindedness

We live in a day and age marked by ever-increasing instability amongst professing Christian people. American society in general has become progressively unstable, and this has a definite effect on those who are named in the name of Christ. There are several examples: one of them is the obvious unrest and moving around that predominates the church scene today. Church shopping and church hopping has become a real problem in the recent years, and this conduct seems to be on the increase. I have had folks tell me that they knew, "beyond a shadow of a doubt," God had called them to a certain local church, only to bail out of that church within a very short period of time for one dubious reason or another. I know a family that has held membership in at least 5 or 6 Baptist churches all in the same geographical location over the past few years, and I won't be surprised when they leave the one they are at right now for something else that suits their carnal liking. They will tell you that God has called them to each and every one of those ministries, but He somehow changed His mind and sent them elsewhere. Certainly there are legitimate reasons for leaving a church; a church that does not follow biblical patterns, engages in compromise, false teaching or corruption is definitely worth leaving, but one should never leave a church for the light and transient reasons without the clear and evident leading of God. One thing is for sure, all this unrest, running to-and-fro and hither-and-yon has increased the instability of our time, and it is hurting our good churches deeply.

There was a time when God-called missionaries went to the field chosen by God, and stayed there all their lives. Back then, it was unusual to hear of missionaries leaving their field of burden unless God specifically ordained otherwise. Most of them did not come off the field unless they became infirm, or old age prohibited them from continuing their work effectively. In recent years, I have seen a change in all of this. I have seen too many modern-day missionaries go to the field and come off the field after a very short period of time, never to return. Some of their testimony always went like this: while they were on deputation, they had an undying burden and love for the country and people God called them to, but once they got to the field and the going got rough, they withdrew, declaring that God had changed their burden, and redirected them to another ministry. Sorry, my friends, but God does not work that way! I am more concerned about a missionary's professed call and his dedication and burden for his field of service when he and his family return to the states after few months or so for any number of reasons. Yes, some may be legitimate, but many are not. I wonder about their professed call, and their heart's dedication to the field where they went to serve. Certainly there are extenuating circumstances when the truly God-called missionary must come off the field, but again, it will not be for light and transient reasons.

Surely, a double-minded man cannot be walking in the spirit, nor can he have the mind of Christ in spiritual things. The double-minded man cannot be a prayer-dependent person, nor is he spiritually sensitive. The double-minded man, in his instability, will always demonstrate poor judgment. He is generally ruled by his emotions and his feelings. He often operates by his own agenda and will declare that God has called or ordained him to do "this or that," and will quickly change what he says God called or ordained him to do when it does not work out to his liking. It is amazing how easily a Christian not walking in the spirit can attribute the things he does outside the will of God to the direct leading of God when He had nothing to do with it. God must be deeply grieved by all of this flip-flopping He sees in His children when double-mindedness replaces the mind of Christ in all that we do. All of this instability is dishonoring to God, and we must, at all costs, take great care to prevent ourselves from being given over to it.

A double-minded man cannot be trusted; his decisions, thinking and ways also cannot be trusted. His instability will have negative and deleterious effect on all and whom he has to do with — this is especially true for those in leadership positions. The leadership of a double-minded man cannot be trusted. The double-minded man will often be given to prevarication as he will tailor what he says and does to fit his wants as opposed to what God wants.

The Christian who is always indecisive and is constantly changing his or her mind does not know or understand what the will of God is. One day they will say that thus-and-thus is God's will for their lives, and the next day, it isn't God's will for their lives anymore; far too many, decisions are based on what they feel is right as opposed to what God clearly said is right. The Word of God is neither applied to any given situation, nor is it the rule for decision-making on the part of the double-minded man. Double-minded and unstable men are always reactionary and their decisions are often experience-driven. I have seen far too many Christian folks make decisions that they vehemently declared to be God's will, and then all of a sudden, it was no longer God's will when things didn't work out as they had planned, wanted or thought they would and should. Who changed? Certainly not God! *"God is not a man, that he should lie; neither the son of man, that he should repent: hath he said, and shall he not do it? or hath he spoken, and shall he not make it good?"* (Numbers 23:19). *"For I am the LORD, I change not; therefore ye sons of Jacob are not consumed"* (Malachi 3:6).

"Reuben, thou art my firstborn, my might, and the beginning of my strength, the excellency of dignity, and the excellency of power: Unstable as water, thou shalt not excel; because thou wentest up to thy father's bed; then defiledst thou it: he went up to my couch." (Genesis 49:3-4). This is just a record of how far instability in a man can take him. Uncorrected personal instability, as it is intrinsic to the flesh, can eventually lead to all sorts of personal downfall which can certainly even lead to acts of immorality. The conduct of Reuben is an outstanding example of how far instability can carry a man given over to it. Double-mindedness and instability is definitely a downward path; it is ruinous to men's integrity and trustworthiness. In his instability, Reuben had no government over his fleshly appetites and he was ruled by his carnal desires. It is sad that unchecked double-mindedness and instability in a man's life can open the doors to some pretty horrible things. One thing is for sure, the unstable man will not excel.

Back in the 1980's, a well-known evangelist was preaching at a conference in one of the major fundamental Christian universities in America. During the course of the conference week, he learned that a very large number of former pastoral theology students had changed their majors to business administration or some other professional course of instruction. This grieved him so much, that he preached several messages aimed at the heart of these young men, impressed upon him by the Lord, to convict them about their double-mindedness. Though he certainly would not have found fault with any student changing his major after discovering he had not been genuinely called to preach, he sensed that many were called to preach, but got their eyes off the Lord, and succumbed to carnal reasoning in their change of direction. Through the faithful preaching of the Word, the power of God fell on the meetings and many young men repented of their double-mindedness; they changed their major back to pastoral theology, missions, or evangelism. Amen, and amen! This certainly pleased the Lord as double-mindedness and instability was conquered in the lives of these good young preachers.

Let me say this in conclusion. Good men with good intentions can make bad decisions and be given to instability when their emotions rule them. All of us have made some very bad decisions in our life at one time or another as a result of transient instability. That is why I always counsel men to never make any decisions when they are upset or when their emotions are running very high. This will surely lead to double-mindedness. The best way is to fast and pray until the emotions are under control and one's spirit is calmed before making any decision that will not only affect you, but will also affect others as well. Let us be aware of the danger of double-mindedness, and flee from it in all of its insidious forms.

CHAPTER FIVE

Single-Mindedness Vs. Double-Mindedness

2 Corinthians 10:5-6 gives us a very important directive. It tells us to "take every thought captive" and to deal with the thoughts that are not of faith. God knows that taking every thought captive is critical because our thoughts are first triggered in the chain-reaction of our souls. In other words, our thoughts stir up our emotions; our emotions then influence our choices; and our choices are what produce our lives. Thus, whoever controls their thinking will ultimately be the one who controls their lives. In this chapter, we want to visually see how this process works and why our choices are very critical. Let's begin by exploring how the Bible defines our mind and see if we can understand a little more clearly why the Lord considers our thoughts very important. According to scripture, our minds are not just our thoughts, reason or intellect, but a whole conceptual process. This

process begins with the spirit that resides at the core of our being and ends with the life that is produced out of our soul. This whole process, according to scripture, is called "mind," or "nous" in Greek. (Romans 12:2)

Three Types of Minds

Scripture speaks about three types of minds: the natural mind (an unbeliever), a double-minded person (a Christian) and a single-minded person (also a Christian).

Lets look at the spirit (which is the power source or the energy source) that creates the thoughts of our hearts. And then, those thoughts are produced out in our lives (or our souls) as actions. In other words, the spirit creates the thoughts of our hearts and those thoughts then produce our life actions. This whole process, according to the Bible, is called our mind.

" The natural man **Mind**", i.e. an unbeliever or one who has no influence from God at all, is going to be a natural, self-centered conceptual process. The process begins with the natural man's spirit, which resides at the core of his being. This spirit creates self-centered thoughts in the natural man's heart, and eventually, self-centered life actions in his soul. For this unbelieving person, there is no choice other than to follow what he naturally thinks or feels because there is no other power source (no other spirit within him) to produce anything different. (1 Corinthians 2:14)

"The Believer's **Mind.**" (someone who has invited Jesus

Christ into his heart) should be a God-centered conceptual process, because God's Spirit dwells at the core of his being. In other words, God's Spirit is the One who creates God-centered thoughts in this person's heart, which should then produce God-centered life actions in his soul. This is God's ideal and perfect will.

This God-centered conceptual process in scripture is called "Single-mindedness." The Greek word is "psyche" means one-souled. Single-mindedness means that only one life being lived here — God's. In other words, God's Life is freely coming forth from this person's heart and is producing Godly life actions in his soul. This is a person who, for the moment, is Spirit-filled and living the truth (his words and deeds match).

A Perfect Example: Single-minded Joseph

An example of someone who was single-minded in the scripture is Joseph in Genesis 39. As you may recall, after Joseph was sold to the Ishmaelites traveling to Egypt, he was assigned to work in the household of Potiphar, an officer of Pharaoh and captain of the guard. Potiphar chose Joseph to be the overseer of his house, because he trusted him completely. Potiphar committed everything into Joseph's hands and God blessed Potiphar because of this action.

Potiphar's wife, however, was not so trustworthy. When Potiphar was gone, she enticed Joseph to lay with her. Joseph refused her offer saying, "How could I do that to Potiphar when he has entrusted everything to me? And besides, how could I sin against God?" Potiphar's wife wouldn't take no for an answer, therefore, she remained persistent. One day, when Joseph went into the house, she physically caught hold of him; as he tried to flee, she ripped off his garment and kept it as evidence against him. She lied to the servants and her husband that evening by saying that Joseph had attacked her. Potiphar was grieved, but he had no other choice but to put Joseph in prison. The Lord adds a footnote to this story in Genesis 39:21, it says that even in prison, "...*the Lord was with Joseph, and showed him mercy and gave him favor...*" It also goes on to say that all who saw Joseph knew God was with him. Joseph, to me, is a perfect example of a person who is single-minded. Even though he was repeatedly tempted, he kept on choosing to give God his thoughts so that God's Life could still freely come forth from his heart. Because of his choice to stay single-minded, Joseph was easily conformed to God's image and everyone who saw him was aware that "God was with him." In other words, he showed forth God's character. Unfortunately, there is another choice for a Christian, and this is where many of us live our entire Christian lives.

"The double-**Mind.**" This is a picture of a believer who has God's thoughts in his heart (he's a Christian), but because he has chosen to follow his own lusts, hurts, frustration, anger (justified or not) and so on, God's Life has been blocked from coming forth, and in its place, self-centered life actions are produced. This is called double-mindedness, or being "twice-souled." It means that two lives are being lived — God's and his own. This, then, is a Christian who is being conformed to the world's image, not Christ's.

An Example: Double-minded David

A perfect scriptural example of double-mindedness is David in 2 Samuel 11. As you recall, David was on the roof of his palace when he saw Bathsheba bathing next door. He thought she was absolutely beautiful, and he wanted her. Rather than cast out those ungodly thoughts as Joseph did, David allowed those lustful thoughts to stir up his emotions, feed his desires and finally influence his actions. David sent his servants to inquire about the woman. They came back and reported that she was Bathsheba, the wife of Uriah. The thought that she was someone else's wife didn't stop David; he was already emotionally wrapped up that he chose to act upon his own desires, sent for Bathsheba and laid with her. When David learned that Bathsheba was pregnant, he called Uriah home, thinking he could cover his sin. Uriah, however, in deference to his men on the front lines of the war, didn't sleep with his wife, but rested on the porch of his house. When David found out that his cover-up had not worked, he commanded that Uriah should be put at the front lines of the battle and that the troops be pulled back from him. Just as David had hoped, Uriah was killed, then David took Bathsheba as his wife. To me, David's behavior presents a perfect example of a double-minded man. Even though he had God's Life in his heart and had been "a man after God's own heart," he still chose to go with the tide and follow the lusts of his own flesh over what God was prompting him to do. (Acts 13:22c)

James 1:14-15 is provocative in light of David's story: "...*every man is tempted, when he is drawn away [from making the right faith choice] by his own lust [a strong desire], and enticed [captured by it]. Then when lust hath conceived [they have made the choice to follow it], it brings forth sin; and sin, when it is finished, brings forth death [separation from God]."* For this short period of time, David lived a lie. His words, "I love God," and his actions obviously did not match. People could no longer see God in him; he had totally given himself over to his own will and desires, and thus, God's Life was quenched.

How Satan revels in our double-mindedness! He knows that double-mindedness will not only keeps us bound by our hurts and wounds, but it also causes the enemies of God to blaspheme. (2 Samuel 12:14) Thus, Satan and all his hordes want us to respond "emotionally."

Consequently, we can be Christians all of our lives with God's Life in our hearts, but because we continue to make emotional choices that follow what we think, feel and desire over what God has prompted us to do, God's Life in us has been quenched. Thus, no one will ever see the difference between our life and that of our neighbors who don't even know who God is. Yes, we are Christians and belong to God but live two different lives under separate influences. God's supernatural life is still in our hearts, but the life that is coming forth from our soul is "self-life," our own thoughts and emotions, and not God's Life at all. Titus 1:16 describes this state perfectly, it states that: *"They profess that they know God [intimately], but in works [actions] they deny Him..."*

CONCLUSION

Throughout scripture, God is alerting us that the battle for our lives is really waged in our minds. We're either going to be single-minded, allowing God's Life into our hearts to motivate and direct all our actions; or double-minded, blocking God's Life in our heart and showing forth "self-life" in our soul.

Which are you?

About Author

Cheryl T. Long is a multi-talented author. A mother of 4 beautiful children and a medical office manager who loves to write and share her stories with all she come in contact with. She had one vision in her mind — to give people around her an imaginable outlet.

More Books by the Author

Love Yourself (Breaking the chains of self doubt)

Facing the Fear on being Alone

How to Deal with the silent treatment

Toxic People who to deal with Them

Letting go of a toxic relationship

Letting Go and Letting God (Ways to surrender control)

Exchange Emotional Pain for Peace and Prosperity

All book available in print and E-book

Stay in touch

www.deardaughterslovesmom. com

www.ingramcontent.com/pod-product-compliance
Lightning Source LLC
Chambersburg PA
CBHW060633030426
42337CB00018B/3336